Cooper's Hawk and Long-Eared Owl Nest Occupancy and Productivity in Piceance Basin, Colorado

Technical Note 442 ⌒ May 2013

Brett Smithers
Wildlife Biologist
Bureau of Land Management
White River Field Office
Meeker, Colorado

Acknowledgments

The author expresses appreciation to Brady Dunne for assisting with data collection and for providing helpful comments regarding the development of this report. Without his ability to work with people and adapt to unique and often stressful situations, the successful outcome of this project would be uncertain. Brady's contribution to this project included many hard-worked hours searching for raptor nests, fighting off biting insects, and providing valuable insight into the daily nesting activities of *Accipiter*. The author also thanks Ed Hollowed, with the Bureau of Land Management's White River Field Office, for his continued interest and support. Lastly, the author extends thanks Dr. Clint Boal, with the Texas Cooperative Fish and Wildlife Research Unit at Texas Tech University, for reviewing various drafts of this document and for providing inspiration to publish this information. Funding for this project was provided by the Bureau of Land Management.

Table of Contents

The purpose of this publication . . . is to expand the current understanding of Cooper's hawk (Accipiter cooperii) and long-eared owl (Asio otus) nesting density, nest occupancy, and productivity information in areas affected by oil and gas development.

Abstract

The purpose of this publication is to convey research findings to the Bureau of Land Management and other federal and state agencies to expand the current understanding of Cooper's hawk (*Accipiter cooperii*) and long-eared owl (*Asio otus*) nesting density, nest occupancy, and productivity information in areas affected by oil and gas development. The Piceance Basin in northwestern Colorado was chosen as the study area because it has a high density of nesting Cooper's hawk and oil and gas exploration, extraction, and production activities. Of the 304 nest structures visited during the 2011 breeding season, 34% were classified as occupied, and 65% were classified as unoccupied. Of the occupied nests in which the outcome of the nesting attempt (i.e., failed, successful, or unknown) was recorded, an observed success rate of 50% and a nest failure rate of 34% was recorded. Consequently, the outcome of the nesting attempt was not recorded at 16% of the monitored nests. When considering all 2011 Cooper's hawk and long-eared owl nesting attempts, fledging rates were 1.3 ($\pm$ 0.23) and 1.4 ($\pm$ 0.36) fledglings produced per nesting attempt, respectively. The number of fledglings produced per nesting attempt among Cooper's hawk and long-eared owl significantly declined from 2010 to 2011; however, there was no statistical difference among occupied Cooper's hawk nests and long-eared owl nests when examining differences in fledging rates at successful nests only. When pooling occupancy data involving several other raptor species, nesting area reoccupancy during the 2011 breeding season was low, with only 29% of occupied areas in 2010 reoccupied in 2011; however, nesting area reoccupancy was high for Cooper's hawk. The results provide additional support of the stochastic nature of nest occupancy and annual reproduction of Cooper's hawk and long-eared owl in northwestern Colorado. To benefit management planning and conservation efforts, these findings suggest additional research is needed to assess the importance of habitat heterogeneity and the ability of Cooper's hawk to maintain overall production of young at a relatively high rate at the site-specific scale, while overall production might be low at the landscape scale.

*The objective of this
publication is to provide a
descriptive summary of
nest occupancy and
productivity information
on a distinct population
of Cooper's hawk
and long-eared owl . . .*

Introduction

Only a small amount of published information relates oil and gas exploration, extraction, and production activities to nest occupancy and productivity of Cooper's hawk (*Accipiter cooperii*) and long-eared owl (*Asio otus*) (Kennedy 1980). Moreover, very little published literature describes Cooper's hawk nesting densities in pinyon-juniper woodlands (Slater and Smith 2010).

In April 2008, the Bureau of Land Management (BLM) White River Field Office received funding via the BLM's competitive Budget Planning System for a project designed to collect breeding season information from woodland raptors in the Piceance Basin, Colorado. The purpose of this project was to collect information that would allow for an assessment of annual reproduction and territory occupancy over time in areas heavily influenced by natural gas exploration and extraction activities. For purposes of statistical comparison, the target species were the Cooper's hawk and long-eared owl.

The objective of this publication is to provide a descriptive summary of nest occupancy and productivity information on a distinct population of Cooper's hawk and long-eared owl that occupy an area of northwestern Colorado where oil and gas development activities have resulted in a patchwork of discrete disturbance features.

*The Piceance Basin
in Rio Blanco County
(northwest Colorado)
was identified as an area
that supports exceptionally
high densities of nesting
Cooper's hawk . . .*

Study Area

The Piceance Basin in Rio Blanco County (northwest Colorado) was identified as an area that supports exceptionally high densities of nesting Cooper's hawk (Smithers 2009). The images in Figure 1 represent typical Cooper's hawk and long-eared owl nesting habitat common throughout the Piceance Basin.

Figure 1. Typical Cooper's hawk and long-eared owl nesting habitat in Piceance Basin

This region of Colorado is also rich in mineral resources, primarily natural gas and oil. Natural gas extraction infrastructure, such as well pads, pipeline and road corridors, compressors, and water treatment facilities, are the dominant anthropogenic disturbance features throughout the study area. See Figure 2. The construction and installation of these facilities, combined with the reclamation and revegetation of these sites through both natural and human-influenced processes, have created a mosaic of mixed-aged vegetative cover classes.

Figure 2. Dominant anthropogenic disturbance features found throughout the study area (beginning with the top photo): treatment facility, vehicle traffic, pipeline installation and vegetation removal, and natural gas well pad

The study area is located in northwestern Colorado, Sixth Principal Meridian, Township 2 N. - 4 S., Range 95 - 100 W., an area ranging from 1,737 to 2,590 m in elevation (Sedgwick 1987). Figure 3 illustrates the geographic extent of the study area (symbolized as a black box) where raptor nest occupancy and productivity information was collected during the 2010 and 2011 breeding seasons in Piceance Basin.

The dominant overstory vegetation in the study area is pinyon pine (*Pinus edulis*) and Utah juniper (*Juniperus osteosperma*). Low-elevation woodlands on shales are dominated by juniper with an understory of scattered prairie Junegrass (*Koeleria macrantha*), bluebunch wheatgrass (*Pseudoroegneria spicata*), needle and thread (*Hesperostipa comata*), bottlebrush squirreltail (*Elymus elymoides*), Indian ricegrass (*Achnatherum hymenoides*), and sometimes stunted antelope bitterbrush (*Purshia tridentata*) and mountain mahogany (*Cercocarpus montanus*). Common forbs

include groundsel (*Senecio* spp.), scarlet gilia (*Gilia aggregata*), penstemon (*Penstemon* spp.), phlox (*Phlox* spp.), and rayless tansyaster (*Haplopappus nuttallii*). Pinyon pine, big sagebrush (*Artemisia tridentata*), and western wheatgrass (*Pascopyrum smithii*) join on sandstone to form a more diverse plant community.

Above 2,100 m, pinyon pine is the predominant tree species, and the shrub layer is composed of big sagebrush, rabbitbrush (*Chrysothamnus* spp.), antelope bitterbrush, and occasionally mountain mahogany, chokecherry (*Prunus virginiana*), and Saskatoon serviceberry (*Amelanchier alnifolia*). Gambel oak (*Quercus gambelii*) is prominent on steep slopes and frequently occurs in shady ravines. The grass-forb community above 2,100 m includes most species found at lower elevations, but percentage ground cover is higher; arrowleaf balsamroot (*Balsamorhiza sagittata*) and lupine (*Lupinus* spp.) are also frequently present.

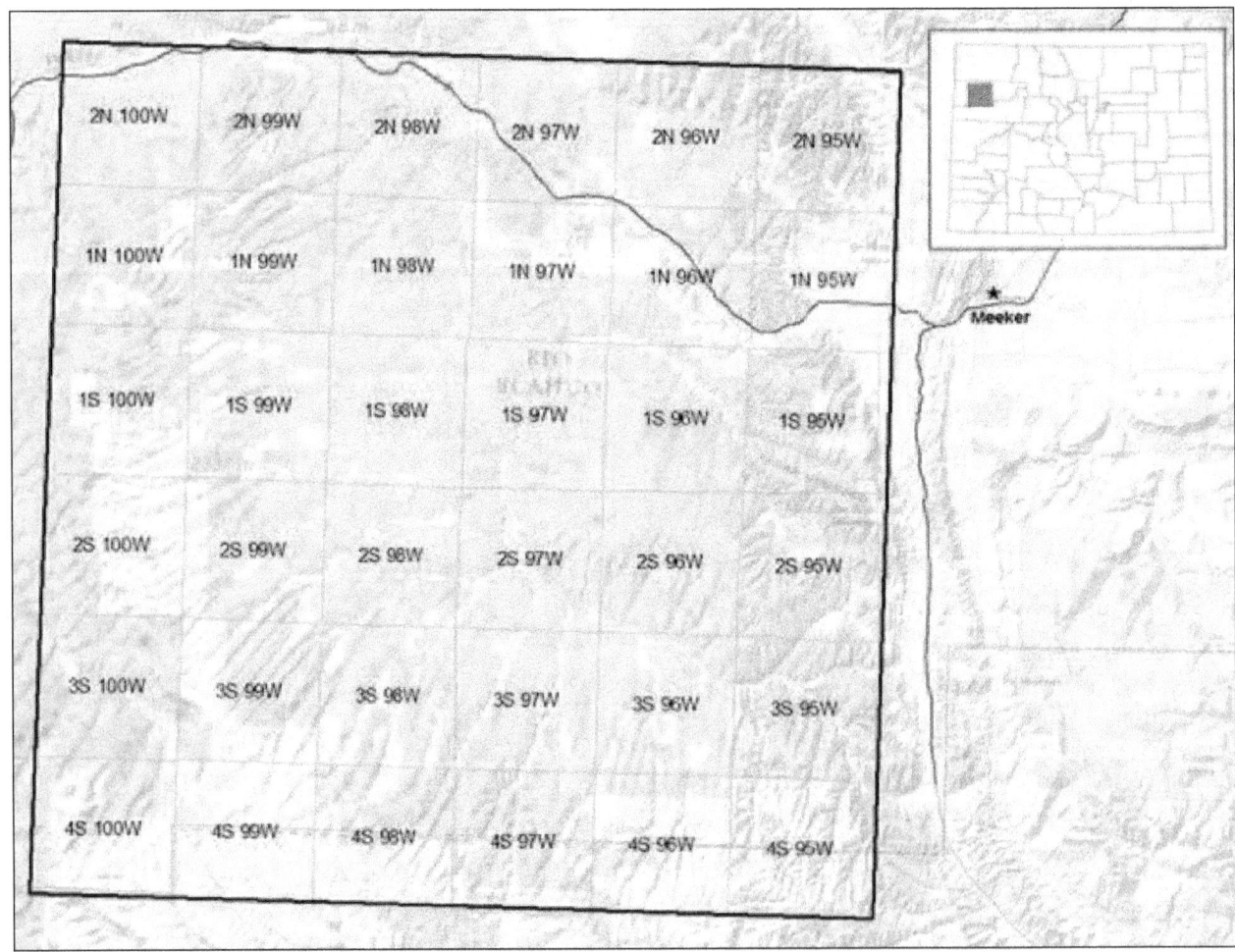

Figure 3. Geographic extent of the study area in Piceance Basin

Methods

Nest Inventory and Monitoring

During the 2008, 2009, 2010, and 2011 accipiter breeding seasons, potential nesting habitat was identified manually using 1-meter resolution National Agriculture Imagery Program (NAIP) imagery and terrain information (e.g., Digital Elevation Model data). Figure 4 illustrates areas that were selected for nest surveys using the 2011 NAIP imagery. The survey areas were identified based on canopy closure, dominant cover type, and tree stem density.

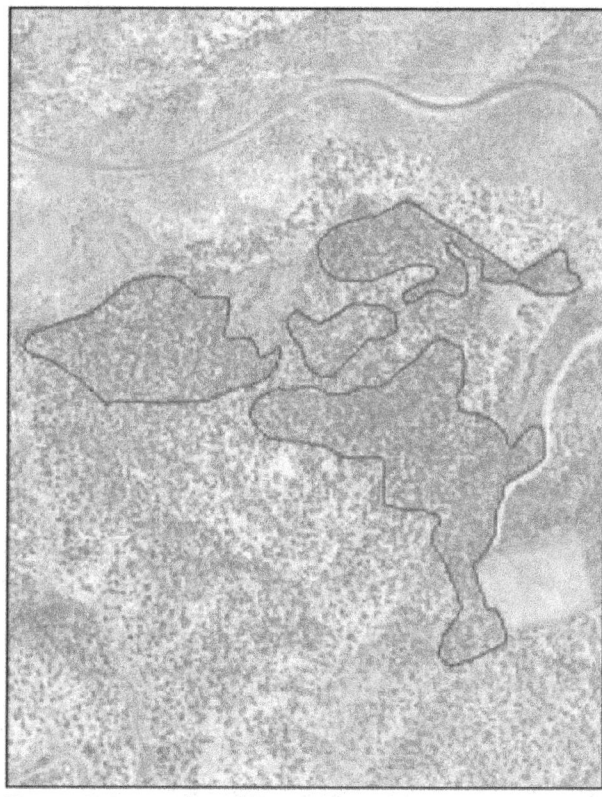

Figure 4. Areas selected for accipiter nest surveys

Monitoring tasks included visiting known nest areas and assessing the breeding season status using procedures outlined in Smithers 2012. Occupancy information was collected opportunistically throughout the study area for all species and pooled together. However, because Cooper's hawk and long-eared owl were the dominant species where these data were collected, the pooled results should be interpreted with caution. Table 1 provides a list of species whose occupancy information was collected.

Table 1. Summary of recorded raptor species and their number of occupied nests in Piceance Basin, Colorado, during the 2011 breeding season

Species	No. Occupied Nests	%
Cooper's hawk	42	40.8
Common raven	18	17.5
Long-eared owl	17	16.5
Red-tailed hawk	13	12.6
Golden eagle	4	3.9
Northern goshawk	3	2.9
Prairie falcon	2	1.9
American kestrel	1	1.0
Bald eagle	1	1.0
Great horned owl	1	1.0
Osprey	1	1.0
Total	**103**	

Known nest structures were relocated using a global positioning system (GPS), specifically a Garmin GPSMAP 76CSx. A Trimble GeoXT GPS unit, with submeter accuracy, was used to further refine position information for all nests in this project. To help navigate to each nest, the Universal Transverse Mercator (UTM) coordinates of each nest were uploaded into the GPS unit using the DNR Garmin version 5.4.1 software. Once at the nest, and to help alleviate any discrepancies between the nest identification number, UTM coordinates, and the actual physical location of the nest, a photo was taken of the GPS screen, in which both the nest ID number and UTM coordinates were displayed. Next, a photo of the nest tree and nest were taken, followed by a closeup photo of the nest and a representative photo of the nest stand. Each series of photos was grouped by the nest ID number and stored in separate folders using the nest ID number as the folder name.

In some cases, the datum was not recorded for a known nest or was unknown. For these nests, a procedure was developed that included converting UTM coordinates from the North American Datum of 1927 (NAD27) to NAD83 or vice versa, while in the field using the Garmin GPSMAP 76CSx unit. For a detailed description of this process, see Smithers 2009. While conducting spring presence/absence surveys, information regarding raptor detections was recorded on the "Nest Monitoring and Raptor Detection Data Form," and ongoing monitoring information collected throughout the breeding season was recorded on the "White River Field Office Nest Monitoring Form" (Smithers 2012).

Known nesting territories from the 2011 accipiter breeding season were monitored from April 24 – September 18, 2011. The start date was the day when full-time nest inventory and monitoring tasks began. The end date was the day when all accipiter juveniles of the nests being monitored had dispersed from the nest stands.

Determining Nest Occupancy

For spring surveys, emphasis was placed on documenting whether or not a nest stand was occupied, rather than evaluating whether the nesting territory was occupied. As such, an "occupied" nest stand included a nest in which either an adult was observed incubating eggs, as suggested by an adult being in an incubating posture on the nest, or by direct observation of eggs in the nest. A "successful" nest was defined as a nest that produced at least one fledgling. Nests that were determined to be occupied during the spring surveys and that did not produce at least one fledgling, for either known or unknown causes, were defined as "failed" nests. For purposes of this research, we define a fledgling as young of the year capable of flying either short distances or capable of sustained flight to and from the nest structure or within the nest stand or post-fledgling area, prior to dispersal from the post-fledgling area.

Nest occupancy was determined based on methods from Steenhof and Newton (2007). Evidence that suggested nests were used during the 2011 breeding season included white streaks of excrement (whitewash) under the nest tree or at the roost site, prey remains in the nest stand, down present on the perimeter of the nest, castings under the nest tree, or fresh nesting material on the nest. According to Smithers (2009, 2010, and 2011), the breeding season status of the nest (i.e., occupied or unoccupied) could be confirmed mid-September due to the amount of residual whitewash that was present under occupied nests. This was true for nests that did not fail during the incubation or early nestling phase, regardless of the amount of young present in the nest during the nestling or fledgling phase. Figure 5 shows whitewash under an occupied Cooper's hawk nest in the study area.

Figure 5. Whitewash under an occupied Cooper's hawk nest in the study area

The condition of individual nests was used as a general guide to assess the status of the nest prior to incubation. Occupied nests most often had fresh material (e.g., branches) and tended to appear less compressed or compacted than unoccupied nests. Unoccupied nests tended to have a flattened or compressed appearance, presumably from the effects of snow compacting nest material during the previous winter (Smithers 2010). Figure 6 shows a typical occupied Cooper's hawk nest in the study area.

Figure 6. Typical occupied Cooper's hawk nest in the study area

All Cooper's hawk and long-eared owl nests that were identified as being occupied during the 2011 spring nest monitoring surveys were visited approximately 17 times throughout the breeding season to assess nest occupancy and predation events, record presence/absence information of adults, and record fledgling dispersal information. Figure 7 provides examples of eggs from the study area that most likely experienced predation events.

Figure 7. Eggs from the study area that most likely experienced predation events (from top to bottom): an egg that was most likely depredated by an avian predator, a membrane still attached to an egg shell, and the jagged edges of an egg shell that was most likely depredated by a mammalian predator

All nest areas that were identified as being occupied during the spring surveys were visited to verify nesting attempt outcomes from June 15 – August 28, 2011. For those nest areas that remained occupied throughout the breeding season, information pertaining to fledging rates and fledging and dispersal dates were recorded for each successful nest.

Nest Reoccupancy Analysis

To complete this analysis, we first selected all occupied 2009 Cooper's hawk nests and exported the nest data to a shapefile. We repeated this process for 2010 and 2011. We then used the near tool to calculate the distance from occupied 2009 Cooper's hawk nests to the nearest occupied 2010 Cooper's hawk nest, using a 500-meter search radius. Nest structures that were reoccupied in 2010 (using the 2009 occupied nests as the near feature) and nest structures that were reoccupied in 2011 (using the 2010 occupied nests as the near feature) resulted in a distance value of zero. The resultant distance values for the 2009/2010 nests were stored in the attribute table of the input file (i.e., the 2010 occupied Cooper's hawk shapefile). We then exported this table to Excel and added the distance values to the data table used for this analysis. We repeated these steps to generate distance values for 2010/2011 nests. Moreover, this process was used to derive distance estimates for reoccupied 2009/2010 and 2010/2011 long-eared owl nests.

The sampling units of this project consisted of nests that were opportunistically selected from a sample of all occupied nests based on accessibility.

Statistical Analysis

The sampling units of this project consisted of nests that were opportunistically selected from a sample of all occupied nests based on accessibility. Thus, nests used in this study were not randomly selected from the population of nests within the study area. All statistical tests were completed using the R statistical software package (R Development Core Team 2005). An alpha of 0.05 was used for all statistical tests, and results are reported as the mean $\pm$ *SE* (standard error).

Because the reoccupancy data were not normally distributed, and because efforts to normalize these data failed, a two-sample, nonparametric Wilcoxan rank sum test (*W*) was used to examine differences in productivity rates, nest reoccupancy distance values, and differences in total precipitation and minimum daily temperatures of the study area in 2010 and 2011.

A total of 304 known raptor nesting territories were visited during the 2011 field season.

Results

Nest Monitoring

A total of 304 known raptor nesting territories were visited during the 2011 field season. Of these nests, 34% ($N = 103$) were classified as being occupied during the spring surveys, and 65% ($N = 198$) of these nests were confirmed as being unoccupied during the 2011 breeding season. Of the occupied nests, the majority were occupied by Cooper's hawk (41%, $N = 42$). For species composition, nest occupancy, and productivity information, see Tables 1, 2, and 3.

Table 2. Summary of 2010 and 2011 success rates of occupied raptor nests in Piceance Basin, Colorado*

	2010				2011			
	N	**Successful**	**Failed**	**Unknown**	**N**	**Successful**	**Failed**	**Unknown**
Occupied	162 (89%)	109 (67%)	15 (9%)	38 (23%)	103 (34%)	52 (50%)	35 (34%)	16 (16%)
Unoccupied	21 (11%)				198 (65%)			
Unknown	0				3 (1%)			
Total	**183**				**304**			

* All percentages are rounded to the nearest percent.

Table 3. Summary of 2010 and 2011 raptor species productivity information in Piceance Basin, Colorado (parentheses indicate 2010 values)

Species	Failed	Successful	Unknown	Total Occupied Nests	No. Fledged (NF)	Mean NF/ Successful Nest	Mean NF/ Nesting Attempt
American kestrel			1 (2)	1 (2)			
Bald eagle	1 (NA)	NA (1)	NA (NA)	1 (1)	NA (1)	NA (1.0)	NA (1.0)
Cooper's hawk	22 (8)	20 (49)	NA (5)	42 (62)	53 (147)	2.7 (3.0)	1.3 (2.4)
Common raven	5 (1)	6 (2)	7 (7)	18 (10)	15 (7)	2.5 (3.5)	0.8 (0.7)
Great horned owl		NA (1)	1 (2)	1 (3)	NA (1)	NA (1)	NA (0.3)
Golden eagle	2 (NA)	2 (1)		4 (1)	2 (1)	1 (1)	0.5 (1)
Long-eared owl	4 (6)	10 (43)	3 (10)	17 (59)	23 (126)	2.3 (2.9)	1.4 (2.1)
Northern goshawk		3 (3)		3 (3)	3 (7)	1.3 (2.3)	1.0 (2.3)
Prairie falcon		2 (2)	NA (1)	2 (3)	3 (2)	1.5 (1)	1.5 (0.7)
Red-tailed hawk	1 (NA)	8 (6)	4 (10)	13 (16)	18 (15)	2.3 (2.5)	1.4 (0.9)
Sharp-shinned hawk		NA (1)		NA (1)	NA (3)	NA (3.0)	NA (3.0)
Saw-whet owl			NA (1)	NA (1)			
Osprey		1 (NA)		1 (NA)	2 (NA)	2.0 (NA)	2.0 (NA)
Total	**35 (15)**	**52 (109)**	**16 (38)**	**103 (162)**	**119 (310)**		

Of the occupied nests in which the outcome of the nesting attempt (i.e., failed or successful) was recorded ($N = 87$ nests), we observed a success rate of 60% ($N = 52$), and a nest failure rate of 40% ($N = 35$) (see Table 2). Compared to 2010 findings, nest failure rates in 2011 represented a 233% increase (15 of 124 nests failed in 2010 vs. 35 of 87 nests failed in 2011). The outcome of 16 nesting attempts ($N = 16$ nests, or 16% of all occupied nests) was not recorded during the 2011 breeding season.

Productivity was similar among Cooper's hawk and long-eared owl in the study area during the 2011 breeding season. When considering only successful (e.g., excluding failed nesting attempts) Cooper's hawk nests (20 of 42 occupied nests in 2011), produced on average 2.7 ($\pm$ 0.20) fledglings per successful nest (see Table 3). This finding was statistically similar to what was recorded in 2010, with 3.0 ($\pm$ 0.14) fledglings produced per successful Cooper's hawk nest ($W = 594.5$, p-value (P) = 0.194). When considering only successful long-eared owl nests, (10 of 17 occupied nests in 2011), an average of 2.3 ($\pm$ 0.30) fledglings were produced per breeding pair. And similar to Cooper's hawk, the number of long-eared owl young produced per successful nest in 2010 and 2011 did not significantly differ ($W = 280$, $P = 0.097$). During the 2010 breeding season, long-eared owl produced an average 2.9 fledglings per successful nest.

Fledging rate information was collected at all nests that successfully fledged young ($N = 52$ successful nests). These nests produced a total of 119 fledglings (an average of 2.3 $\pm$ 0.14 fledglings produced per successful nest). This represents an 18% decline in the number of fledglings produced per successful nest in 2010 ($N = 310$). When considering all occupied nests of all species in 2011, fledging rates within the study area were 1.2 fledglings produced per nesting attempt ($N = 103$ occupied nests). Compared to 2010 findings, only 38% of the total number of fledglings produced in 2010 were produced in 2011.

When considering all Cooper's hawk and long-eared owl nesting attempts (i.e., including both successful and failed nesting attempts), fledging rates were 1.3 (± 0.23) and 1.4 (± 0.36) fledglings produced per nesting attempt, respectively, in the study area (see Table 3). When assessing productivity on the basis of nesting attempts, not just successful nests, we documented a significant decline in the number of fledglings produced per nesting attempt among Cooper's hawk ($W = 1782.5$, $P = 0.00005$) and long-eared owl ($W = 460$, $P = 0.034$) from the 2010 to the 2011 breeding season.

Nest Stand Reoccupancy Analysis

During the 2011 breeding season, occupancy information was collected at an additional 114 nest territories compared to 2010, representing a 67% increase in the number of known nesting territories in the study area from 2010 to 2011 where monitoring information was collected.

Of the nest structures that were occupied in 2010, 136 out of 162 (84%) were visited in 2011. Nest structure reoccupancy during the 2011 breeding season was low, with only 29% ($N = 40$) of nest structures occupied in 2010, and consequently visited in 2011 ($N = 136$), also being reoccupied in 2011. Of the nesting areas that were occupied in 2010, 59% ($N = 96$) were determined to be unoccupied in 2011. Fourteen nests that failed in 2010 ($N = 15$) were visited in 2011. All of the 14 nests were occupied in 2011; however, only 14% ($N = 2$ nests) successfully produced young during the 2011 breeding season. Twenty-six nests (16%) that were occupied in 2010 ($N = 162$) were not revisited in 2011.

Nesting area reoccupancy was high for Cooper's hawk, with 11 pairs (26% of all known 2011 Cooper's hawk territories, $N = 42$) returning to the nest structure that was used in 2010. Additionally, 20 pairs returned to the same nest stand to either construct a new nest or occupy an alternate nest. This calculates to a total of 31 pairs (or 74% of all known 2011 Cooper's hawk territories) reoccupying known nesting territories (e.g., nesting areas) during the 2011 breeding season.

The mean distance between 2010 and 2011 occupied Cooper's hawk nests was 177 m (± 18.9 m, $N = 20$ nest pairs, range = 33.8 to 340.2 m) (see Table 4). The mean distance between 2009 and 2010 occupied Cooper's hawk nests was 186 m (± 43.2 m, $N = 7$, range = 115.4 to 436.2 m). The mean distance between 2009 and 2010 Cooper's hawk nests and 2010 and 2011 Cooper's hawk nests did not significantly differ ($W = 66.5$, $P = 0.8681$).

Table 4 shows the data that was used to compare nest reoccupancy information for Cooper's hawk and long-eared owl in the study area. Cooper's hawk tended to reoccupy or construct nests during the 2011 breeding season that were closer to 2010 occupied nests when compared to those nests that were reoccupied or constructed in 2010 from the 2009 occupied nests, though this relationship was not statistically significant ($W = 66.5$, $P = 0.8681$). Long-eared owl tended to reoccupy or construct nests during the 2011 breeding season that were farther from occupied 2010 nests, when compared to the distance between occupied 2009 and 2010 nests ($W = 31.5$, $P = 0.02807$).

Table 4. Summary of distances (in meters) of occupied Cooper's hawk and long-eared owl nests from 2009 to 2010 and from 2010 to 2011

	Distances Between 2009 and 2010 Occupied Cooper's Hawk Nests	Distances Between 2010 and 2011 Occupied Cooper's Hawk Nests	Distances Between 2009 and 2010 Occupied Long-Eared Owl Nests	Distances Between 2010 and 2011 Occupied Long-Eared Owl Nests
	436.22	113.07	23.71	240.35
	115.43	185.65	61.72	262.55
	115.68	317.41	101.24	290.11
	117.59	252.87	181.39	291.53
	150.22	223.45	291.53	333.67
	181.60	38.47		433.28
	181.95	230.42		436.22
		33.84		
		129.56		
		178.94		
		108.19		
		138.96		
		93.56		
		340.21		
		124.33		
		234.13		
		224.72		
		150.22		
		276.15		
		145.17		
Mean =	185.53	176.97	131.92	326.82
Standard Deviation (SD) =	114.40	84.68	106.66	79.11
Standard Error (SE) =	43.24	18.94	47.70	29.90
Coefficient of Variation (CV) =	0.62	0.48	0.81	0.24
Population Size (N) =	7	20	5	7

Discussion

Although a causal relationship was not discovered for increased nest failure rates during the 2011 breeding season, one factor that could have influenced nest failure rates from 2010 to 2011 is stochastic spring weather events (e.g., rain and snow showers) and cold temperatures (see Figures 8, 9, and 10). Estimated nest failure dates showed that most failures occurred during the months of April and May, which also coincided with early spring rain, snow showers, and cold temperatures. Data used to develop these figures was obtained from the Pinto Ridge Remote Automated Weather Station, which is located in northwest Colorado.

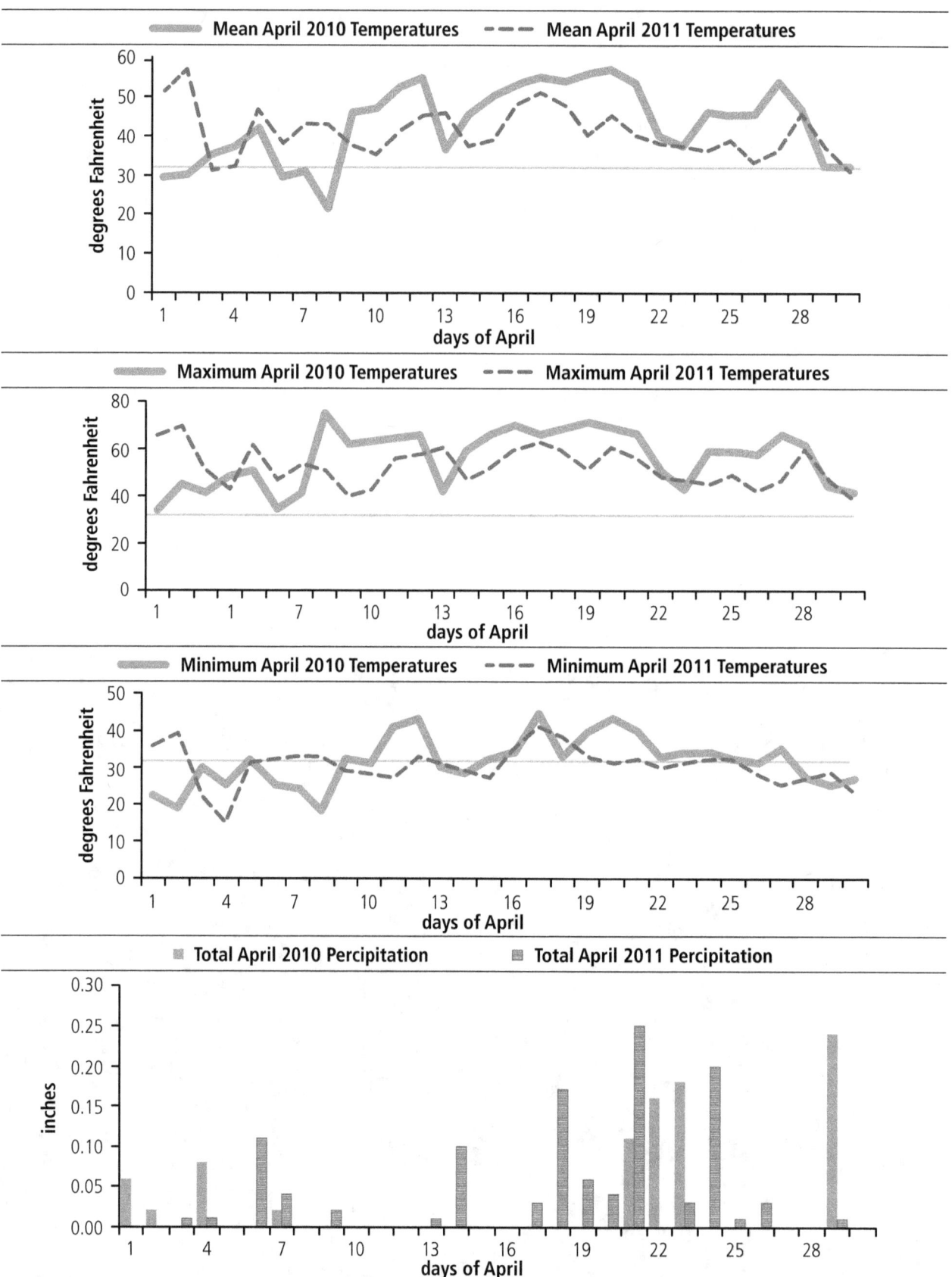

Figure 8. Comparison of April 2010 and April 2011 mean, maximum, and minimum temperatures and precipitation events in the study area

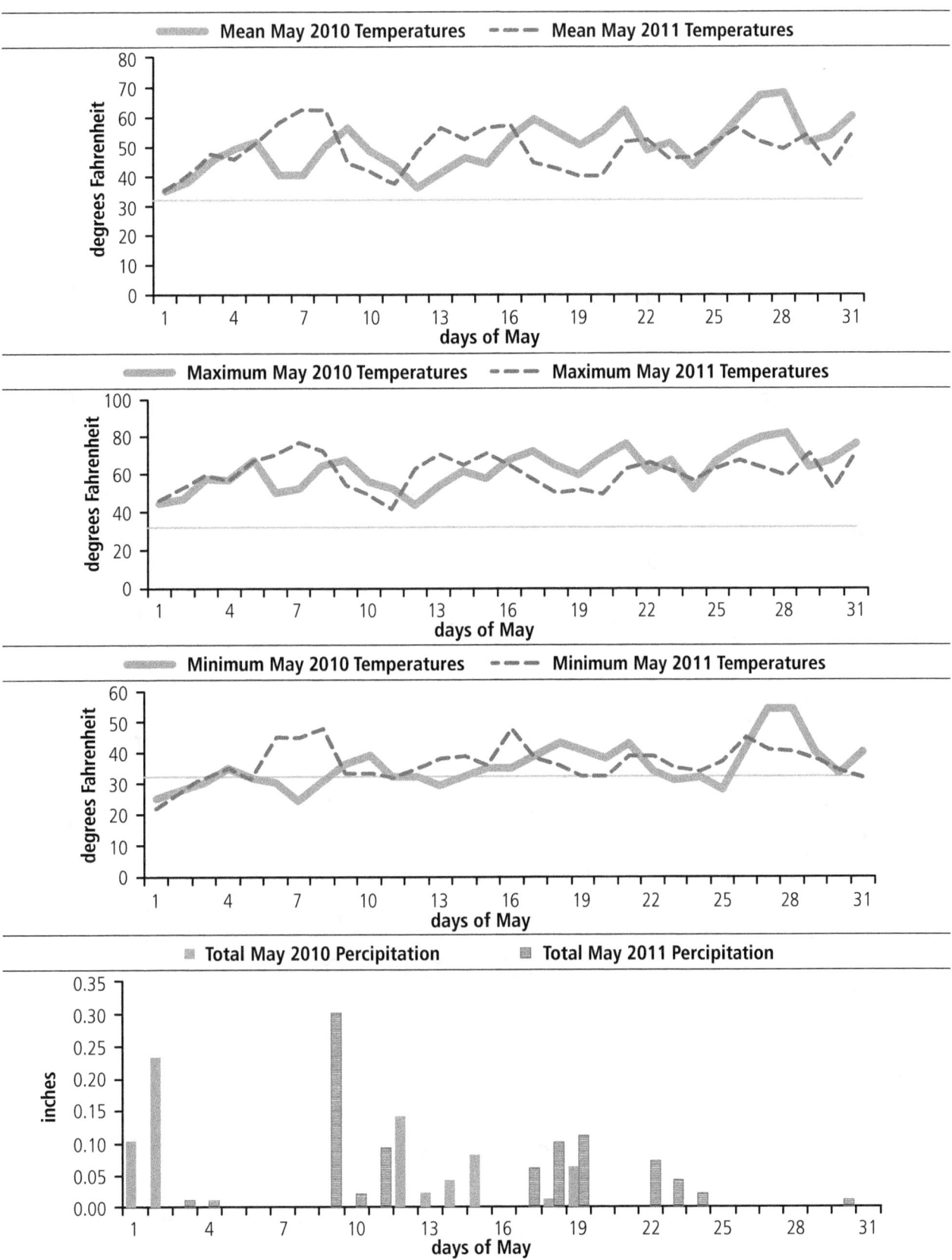

Figure 9. Comparison of May 2010 and May 2011 mean, maximum, and minimum temperatures and precipitation events in the study area

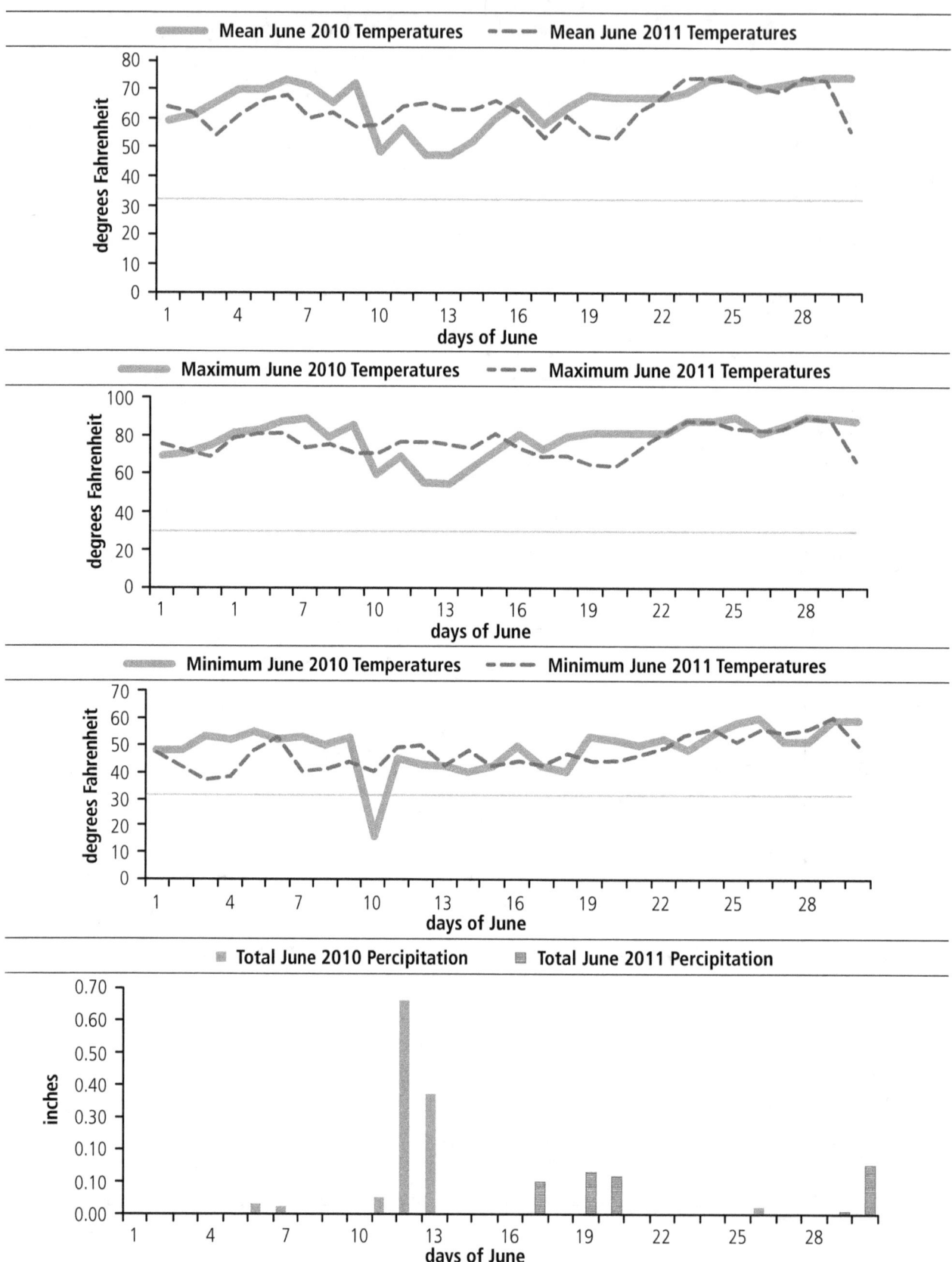

Figure 10. Comparison of June 2010 and June 2011 mean, maximum, and minimum temperatures and precipitation events in the study area

Mean, maximum, and minimum temperatures during April 2011 were generally lower compared to April 2010 temperatures. Moreover, precipitation events in April 2011 were more numerous and more equitably distributed (i.e., precipitation events were distributed equally throughout the month) compared to April 2010 (see Figure 8).

After reviewing the temperature and precipitation information, the only item that stood out was the number of days in which a measureable amount of precipitation was recorded during the month of April 2011. In April 2010, there were a total of 8 days in which a measurable amount of precipitation was recorded, compared to 17 days in April 2011; however, total precipitation did not significantly differ between April 2010 and April 2011 ($W = 93$, $P = 0.15$), with 0.87 and 1.13 in, respectively. Also, mean values for minimum temperatures did not significantly differ between April 2010 and April 2011 ($W = 490.5$, $P = 0.55$), with 32 and 30° F, respectively. Although there was no statistical difference in mean April precipitation estimates between years, findings suggest that the distribution of precipitation events may influence Cooper's hawk nest productivity more than the total volume of precipitation produced per event.

Unfortunately, prey delivery rates were not assessed during the 2011 breeding season. However, based on anecdotal evidence, and using the same observer in 2011 as 2010, there was a noticed decline in the overall presence of either adult in the nest stand during routine monitoring visits. In addition, unlike observations recorded during the 2010 breeding season at occupied nests, during the 2011 breeding season, a measurable decline was noticed in the number of occurrences in which prey items were observed on the rim of the nest, in the nesting area, or on the ground directly below the nest. See Figure 10.

Moreover, when compared to 2010 observations, fledglings tended to disperse from the nest stand, and presumably from the post fledging area, sooner in 2011 than in 2010. These anecdotal observations suggest that prey abundance and possibly prey availability may have been reduced during the 2011 breeding season, which may have also influenced nest occupancy and productivity results.

In 2011, fledging rate information was collected at all successful nests ($N = 52$), though these data are heavily skewed towards Cooper's hawk ($N = 20$) and long-eared owl ($N = 10$). Of those nests that

Figure 10. Uneaten prey found below two occupied Cooper's hawk nests in 2010 in the study area

were successful, a total of 119 fledglings (an average of 2.3 ± 0.14 fledglings produced per successful nest), represents an 18% decline in the number of fledglings produced per successful nest in 2010 ($N = 310$). When considering all occupied nests for all species in 2011, fledging rates within the study area were 1.2 fledglings produced per nesting attempt ($N = 103$ occupied nests). Compared to 2010 findings, only 38% of the total number of fledglings produced in 2010 ($N = 310$ fledglings) were produced in 2011 (see Table 3).

Because the same observer was used in both 2010 and 2011, and because the amount of survey effort was similar during the 2010 and 2011 breeding seasons, we are led to believe that there was both a numerical and biological difference (i.e., decline) in the number of fledglings produced per successful nest in 2011 compared to 2010. Also, as mentioned previously, both seasonal weather patterns and prey abundance and prey availability most likely led to the observed pattern.

Compared to 2010 findings, productivity was similar among Cooper's hawk and long-eared owl for successful nests in the study area during the 2011 breeding season. When considering 2011 successful Cooper's hawk nests ($N = 20$), Cooper's hawk produced an average 2.7 ($\pm$ 0.20) fledglings, which is statistically similar to what was recorded in 2010, with 3.0 ($\pm$ 0.14) fledglings produced per successful nest ($W = 594.5, P = 0.194$). This finding contradicts our supposition that prey abundance and availability might have been a key factor influencing nest occupancy and productivity results. If prey availability and abundance was a primary factor influencing nest occupancy and productivity results, then one would expect a noticeable decline in the number of fledglings produced per successful nest when looking at all successful Cooper's hawk nests. However, this finding provides support for the clustered distribution of occupied Cooper's hawk nests as it relates to prey abundance and availability, which is most likely also clustered and patchy during years when prey density is low. Cooper's hawk nest occupancy and productivity may be more heavily influenced by the distribution, abundance, and availability of small mammals in the study area.

Based on nest occupancy and productivity information, findings recorded in 2010 most likely represent an exceptional year for Cooper's hawk nest occupancy and productivity, and findings recorded in 2011 most likely represent a low year for Cooper's hawk nest occupancy and productivity. When comparing 2010 and 2011 results, 2011 findings provide support for the theory that even though nest occupancy may be low in years when prey densities are low, because of the patchy distribution of prey (both avian and mammalian) within a territory, nest productivity can still be high at the local scale, though nest occupancy and productivity estimates based on the number of fledglings produced per nesting attempt will be low at the regional scale. Additional support of this concept includes the fact that a significant decline was documented in the number of fledglings produced per nesting attempt among occupied Cooper's hawk nests ($W = 1782.5, P = 0.00005$) and long-eared owl nests ($W = 460, P = 0.034$) from the 2010 to the 2011 breeding season.

During the 2011 breeding season, occupancy information was collected at an additional 114 nest territories compared to 2010, representing a 67% increase in the number of known nesting territories in the study area from 2010 to 2011 where monitoring information was collected. This finding can best be explained by the fact that the individual responsible for monitoring nests had more time to visit additional known nest locations and confirm occupancy status because of low nest occupancy and high nest failure rates in the study area. It would have required more time to conduct routine visits to confirm occupancy status if the latter had been true (i.e., higher occupancy rates and lower nest failure rates). As such, these findings do not represent a statistical increase in the number of new territories in the study area. Rather, these findings illustrate a decreased level of effort required to confirm occupancy status when overall nest occupancy is low and nest failure rates are high in the study area.

Literature Cited

Kennedy, P.L. 1980. Raptor baseline studies in energy development. Wildlife Society Bulletin 8 (2): 129-135.

R Development Core Team. 2010. R: A language and environment for statistical computing. ISBN 3-900051-07-0. R Foundation for Statistical Computing, Vienna, Austria. http://www.lsw.uni-heidelberg.de/users/christlieb/teaching/UKStaSS10/R-refman.pdf.

Sedgwick, J.A. 1987. Avian habitat relationships in pinyon-juniper woodland. The Wilson Bulletin 99 (3): 413-431.

Slater, S.J., and J.P. Smith. 2010. Accipiter use of pinyon-juniper habitats for nesting in northwestern Colorado. Tech Note 435. HawkWatch International, Salt Lake City, UT.

Smithers, B.L. 2009. 2009 White River Field Office Raptor Inventory and Monitoring Report. Bureau of Land Management, White River Field Office, Meeker, CO.

Smithers, B.L. 2010. 2010 White River Field Office Raptor Nesting Productivity and Nest Monitoring Report for Piceance Basin, Colorado. Bureau of Land Management, White River Field Office, Meeker, CO.

Smithers, B.L. 2012. White River Field Office Diurnal Raptor Survey Protocol, Version 01/25/12. Bureau of Land Management, White River Field Office, Meeker, CO. http://www.blm.gov/co/st/en/fo/wrfo/wildlife0.html.

Smithers, B.L. In progress. An assessment of Cooper's hawk food habits using video monitoring equipment. Bureau of Land Management, White River Field Office, Meeker, CO.

Steenhof, K., and I. Newton. 2007. Assessing Nesting Success and Productivity. p. 181-191. In: Bird, D.M., and K.L. Bildstein (eds). Raptor Research and Management Techniques, Hancock House, Blaine, WA.

Based on nest occupancy and productivity information, findings recorded in 2010 most likely represent an exceptional year . . . and findings recorded in 2011 most likely represent a low year for Cooper's hawk nest occupancy and productivity.